Fun Facts

The big book of fun and unbelievable facts that will blow your mind!

Table of Contents

Introduction 1

Chapter 1: Fun Facts 2

Conclusion 50

Introduction

Thank you for taking the time to pick up this book, full of fun and unbelievable facts about absolutely everything!

In the following pages, you will find hundreds of the strangest, most interesting, and unbelievable facts.

With the new knowledge you'll learn, you'll be able to wow your friends and family with a variety of weird and wacky facts!

Once again, thanks for choosing this book. I hope you enjoy it!

Chapter 1: Fun Facts

1. North Korea and Cuba are the only countries in the world where you can't buy Coca Cola.

2. Philippines has the shortest population of people in the world, with an average height of 5 feet and 1.8 inches.

3. The Netherlands has the tallest population of people in the world, with an average height of 6 feet.

4. The world's most quiet room is located at Microsoft's headquarters in Washington State. The room was designed specifically to be quiet, and measures a background noise of -20.35 dBa, which is 20 decibels below the threshold of human hearing!

5. Only 3 countries don't use the metric system; the USA, Liberia, and Myanmar.

6. The suburb with the longest name in the world has 85 letters! The town is named **Taumatawhakatangihanga-koauauotamateaturipukakapikimaung-ahoronukupokaiwhenuakitanatahu**, and is located in New Zealand.

7. Four babies are born every single second.

8. The average person will spend 6 months of their life waiting for red traffic lights to turn green.

9. A blue whale's heartbeat can be heard from up to 2-miles away.

10. A lightning bolt contains enough energy to toast 100,000 pieces of bread.

11. Victorians said 'prunes' instead of 'cheese' when taking a photo. Victorian-era people considered smiling in photos to be uncivilized, and something that was reserved for the poor. So, they said 'prunes' as it would help them to avoid smiling and look serious.

12. The world's largest pyramid is in Mexico, not in Egypt! The Great Pyramid of Cholula has a base 4 times the size of the Great Pyramid of Giza.

13. The expiration date on bottled water is for the bottles themselves, not the water. After expiration, the plastic will start leaching into the water.

14. On average, South Koreans are 4cm taller than North Koreans.

15. NASCAR racecar drivers lose up to 10lbs during a race due to sweating!

16. The funny bone is actually a nerve called the ulnar nerve, which is responsible for telling the brain about feelings in the ring and pinkie fingers.

17. The most widely printed book in the world is the Ikea catalog. The catalog is printed 200-million times each year, which is more than the Bible, the Quran, and the entire Harry Potter series.

18. When you crack your knuckles, the noise is made by gases being released. These gases are trapped between the joints and are released when you 'crack' your knuckles.

19. The largest snowflake in recorded history was 15-inches wide!

20. Japan experiences more earthquakes than any other country.

21. The most popular name in the world is Muhammad. This is thanks to the Muslim tradition of naming the first-born son after Muhammad, the Islamic prophet.

22. Only two countries use the color purple in their flag. The countries are Nicaragua and Dominica.

23. The world's most expensive coin was sold for more than $7-million dollars. The $20 US coin was made in 1933 and never put into circulation. A limited number were made, and most were destroyed, except for nine that were presumed to be stolen. One of these remaining coins was sold at auction in 2002 for $7,590,020!

24. South Sudan is the youngest country in the world. South Sudan only gained its independence in 2011 when it separated from Sudan.

25. Only 12.3% of the world's population is aged 60 and over.

26. Sweden has more islands than any other country in the world. Of their 221,800 islands, only about 1,000 are inhabited!

27. The combination of a question mark and an exclamation mark '?!' is called an interrobang and was invented in the 1960s by an advertiser named Martin Speckter.

28. It is illegal to own only one guinea pig in Switzerland. Guinea pigs are pack animals and get depressed if they live alone. As a result, Switzerland classifies owning just one guinea pig to be an act of animal cruelty.

29. The first written 'OMG' was used in a letter to Winston Churchill in 1917.

30. Flipping a shark upside down immobilizes it for up to 15 minutes. This is due to the loosening of muscles and the respiratory system, making the shark enter a state of immobility. Some killer whales make use of this fact by flipping sharks, making it easier for them to access prey.

31. The Beauty and the Beast was originally written to help girls accept arranged marriages. The original story was written in 1740, by French author Gabrielle-Suzanne Barbot de Villeneuve.

32. Evidence suggest that plants have existed on dry land for at least 450-million years!

33. Australia has more than 10,000 different beaches. You could visit a different beach every day for 27 years!

34. The national animal of Scotland is the unicorn.

35. Sloths have been observed to occasionally mistake their own arm for a branch and fall to their deaths.

36. There is an uninhabited island in the Bahamas that is entirely populated by swimming pigs. It's appropriately known as 'Pig Beach'.

37. Catnip is ten times more effective at repelling mosquitos than DEET, the main ingredient in most bug repellents.

38. In the early 1900s, lobster was considered to be a food reserved for poor people and was often eaten by the homeless. It wasn't until after World War II that it became popular with the upper class!

39. Rabbits are born hairless and blind. Hares on the other hand are born with fur and can see.

40. The world's largest pineapple was grown by an Australian named Christine McCallum. The pineapple was an impressive 32cm (12.6-inches) long and weighed in at 8.28KG (18.25lbs)!

41. Surgeons who play video games for 3 hours or more per week have been shown to perform 27% faster than their peers, and make 37% fewer mistakes!

42. The word 'almost' is the longest word in the English language to have all of its letters appear in alphabetical order.

43. The world's biggest turtle was discovered in Wales in 1988. It was 9 foot in length and weighed in at a whopping 2,016lbs!

44. 2013 was the first year since 1987 to feature four different numbers.

45. Butterflies taste with their hind feet.

46. A group of crows is referred to as 'a murder'.

47. India considers cows to be a sacred animal, and even has a Bill of Rights for cows.

48. According to their DNA, the children of identical twins are technically half-siblings, not cousins! Cousins normally share 12.5% of the same DNA, but with the children of identical twins, that becomes 25%.

49. A cornflake that was shaped like Illinois was sold in eBay in 2008 for $1,350!

50. Based on their size and water density, clouds often weigh more than one-million-pounds!

51. According to British law, any unclaimed swan swimming in the open waters of England or Wales is the property of the Queen!

52. Blood donors in Sweden are notified via text when their blood is used.

53. Tug of war was once an event at the Olympics.

54. Bumblebees can fly higher than Mount Everest!

55. The world's tallest dog was a Great Dane named Zeus that stood at an impressive 7'4 when upright!

56. In ancient times, spider webs were used as bandages.

57. Colombian drug-lord Pablo Escobar purchased 4 hippos for his personal zoo. After his death, the hippos escaped and have since bred. Now, there are more than 40 wild hippos in Colombia!

58. It is estimated that there are over 20-million different species of animal in the Amazon rainforest!

59. There is no specific time zone at the South Pole, because it's the point that all longitude points meet. The stations on the South Pole use the time zone of the country that owns them.

60. The biggest type of Pterodactyl had a wingspan of roughly 39-foot! That's bigger than the wingspan of an F16 fighter jet.

61. The Burj Khalifa is the world's tallest building, standing at a staggering 830 meters (2,723 feet). It's so tall that you can watch the sunset from the ground, take an elevator to the top, and then watch the sunset all over again!

62. Bowler hats were originally designed to be safety hats to help protect horse riders from hitting their head on branches.

63. Armadillo shells are so hard that they can deflect a bullet!

64. Antarctica is the world's largest desert, spanning roughly 5.5-million square miles.

65. Your ears and nose are the only parts of your body that never stop growing.

66. Due to heat causing the metal to expand, the Eiffel tower 'grows' by up to 6-inches during Summer!

67. Up until 2015, it was illegal to dance in Japan after midnight.

68. In England, pigeon poop is the property of the Crown. It was once used to make gunpower, and as a result King George declared all pigeon poop to be the property of the Crown in the 18th century!

69. The letter 'E' is the most used letter in the English language, appearing in roughly 11% of all words.

70. Female gladiators fought alongside their male counterparts and were known as Gladiatrix.

71. Koalas, Chimpanzees, and Gorillas all have unique fingerprints. Koala fingerprints are so similar to humans that it's almost impossible to tell them apart!

72. A species of shark called 'Greenland Sharks' can live for up to 500 years!

73. Natural bananas have loads of seeds in them! The bananas you find in the store are nice and seed free thanks to selective breeding over many generations.

74. All astronauts that go to the International Space Station have to learn Russian, because to get to the ISS they must travel in a Russian spacecraft.

75. Thanks to their small weight and tough exoskeleton, ants can't die from being dropped – even if they were to be dropped off of the Empire State Building, they would walk away unscathed!

76. Deep fried chicken originated in Scotland and was brought to America by Scottish immigrants.

77. 40-million years ago there existed a species of giant penguin that stood at 6 feet tall!

78. Before 2011, every drink in Russia under 10% alcohol was classified as soft drink.

79. 25% of all mammal species on earth are bats.

80. The electric chair was invented by a dentist in 1890.

81. Jellyfish are 95% water.

82. There are 3 different species of bird in Australia that deliberately spread fires. They pick up flaming sticks and drop them to spread fires in an attempt to flush out their prey.

83. Italy has 34 different native languages in use today.

84. The Hawaiian flag is a combination of both the American and British flags and was purposely designed that way in 1812 to appeal to both the British and Americans.

85. NASA has internet speeds of 91GB per second!

86. In 1783, a volcanic explosion just south of Iceland killed 25% of the world's human population, and 80% of sheep!

87. The US has more millionaires than Sweden has people!

88. Pteronophobia is the fear of being tickled by feathers.

89. The 29th of May is 'Put a pillow on your fridge day' and is celebrated in Europe and the USA to bring luck to the household!

90. 7% of American adults believe that chocolate milk comes from brown cows.

91. Bananas are curved because they grow towards the sun.

92. An average person produces enough saliva in their lifetime to fill two swimming pools!

93. Movie trailers were originally shown at the end of films, which is how they got the name "trailers".

94. Heart attacks are 20% more likely to happen on a Monday than any other day of the week!

95. In 2017, more people died while taking selfies than were killed by sharks.

96. A lion's roar is so loud that it can be heard up to 5-miles away!

97. The following sentence can be read both backwards and forwards: "Do geese see God?"

98. In Uganda, 48% of the population is under 15 years old, and 77% is under 30!

99. Approximately 10-20% of power outages in the U.S. are caused by squirrels.

100. Facebook, Instagram, and Twitter are all banned in China.

101. Honeybees can recognize human faces.

102. Nearly 3% of the ice in Antarctic glaciers is penguin urine.

103. Bob Dylan's real name is Robert Zimmerman.

104. Crocodiles can't stick their tongues out, but alligators can!

105. Sea otters hold hands while sleeping so they don't drift away from each other.

106. Blue whales are so big that a small child would be able to swim in their veins!

107. There are 1,710 steps in the Eiffel Tower!

108. Pirates wore earrings out of the superstitious belief that it would improve their eyesight and protect them from seasickness and drowning!

109. The Twitter bird is named Larry, after NBA legend Larry Bird.

110. Mike Tyson once offered a zookeeper $10,000 to let him fight a gorilla. Luckily, the zookeeper declined the offer.

111. Vincent Van Gogh only sold one painting during his lifetime. It wasn't until after his death that his artwork became popular and valuable.

112. The average person walks 110,000 miles in their lifetime, which is the equivalent of walking around the world 5 times!

113. Tears contain a natural painkiller that also improves your mood!

114. In the 1800s, ketchup was sold as medicine to help treat indigestion!

115. Ironically, the name for the fear of long words is Hippopotomonstrosesquippedaliophobia.

116. Cows have accents. The way a cow moos differs between herds and locations!

117. You're twice as likely to die from a vending machine falling on you than by being eaten by a shark.

118. The blob of toothpaste on your toothbrush is known as a "nurdle".

119. There's a village in Norway named "hell", and as you would expect, every winter it freezes over!

120. Lobsters communicate by urinating at each other.

121. High heels were originally made for men. In the 15th century they were used by Persian men to help keep their feet secure in their stirrups when horse riding!

122. Polar bear liver is toxic to humans due to its high levels of vitamin A. Even a small amount could be fatal!

123. Saudi Arabia imports camels from Australia. Despite not being native, Australia currently has the largest wild population of camels.

124. When a person gets a kidney transplant, the old kidneys are usually left in the body. This means there are people out there with 3 and 4 kidneys in their body, instead of the usual 2!

125. A moose can dive up to 20 feet underwater in search of food.

126. An octopus has 3 hearts.

127. The first man to fly, and the first man to walk on the moon were alive at the same time! Neil Armstrong was 17 years old when Orville Wright died.

128. The brother of John Wilkes Booth saved the son of Abraham Lincoln from being hit by a train, without knowing who he was!

129. Russia has a greater surface area than Pluto.

130. On Saturn and Jupiter, it rains diamonds!

131. Humans share 50% of their DNA with bananas!

132. The current U.S. flag was designed by Robert G. Heft as a school project when he was 17 years old. He received a B-.

133. Fortune cookies were invented in America – not China.

134. In a room of 23 people, there's a 50-50 chance that two of those people share a birthday! This is known as the birthday paradox.

135. Hippopotamus milk is pink.

136. 16-years of footage is uploaded to YouTube every single day.

137. Of the first 5 U.S. Presidents, 3 of them died on the 4th of July.

138. Cows have best friends and get sad if they are separated for too long.

139. Wooly Mammoths were still alive when the Great Pyramid was being built.

140. If you could double your money every day, and started with a penny, you'd be a millionaire in less than a month.

141. Can openers weren't invented until 50 years after the can was invented.

142. The high five first became popular in 1977 after Dodger player Dusty Baker high fived a teammate after hitting his 30th home run for the season!

143. Chewing gum is illegal in Singapore.

144. Jelly beans take between 6 and 10 days to make, depending on their flavor.

145. There is a psychological disorder called Boanthropy that makes people believe that they are a cow.

146. There is a McDonald's in every continent except for Antarctica!

147. Mr. Potato Head was the first toy to ever be advertised on TV.

148. A duel between three people is known as a truel.

149. Snails have up to 15,000 teeth!

150. Most toilet paper sold in France is pink.

151. The human nose can remember 50,000 scents!

152. 8 of the 10 largest statues in the world are of Buddha.

153. If you sneeze while travelling at 60Mph, your eyes will be closed for approximately 50 feet!

154. Magpie are considered to be one of the world's smartest animals and are one of the few animals that can recognize themselves in a mirror.

155. Baked beans are actually not baked – they're stewed.

156. Sunsets on Mars are blue.

157. The most popular item at Walmart is bananas. They sell more bananas than any other product.

158. 'Digging a hole to China' is theoretically possible if you start in Argentina.

159. As of 1998, 50% of Iceland's population believed in Elves.

160. In Slovakia, many people have a carp live in their bathtub for several days before eating it at Christmas.

161. In Japan, you have the same chance of being struck by lightning as you have of being shot by a gun!

162. Although Australia has the largest number of venomous snakes in the world, it averages only 1 fatal snake bite per year!

163. Sloths can hold their breath longer than dolphins can.

164. It's impossible to hum while holding your nose.

165. Dueling is legal in Paraguay so long as both members are registered blood donors.

166. There are 336 dimples on a regulation golf ball.

167. At any given time, there are roughly 1,800 thunderstorms going on around the world.

168. A "jiffy" is an actual unit of time – it's $1/100^{th}$ of a second.

169. Leonardo Da Vinci invented scissors.

170. An average of 100 people die each year as a result of choking on ball point pens.

171. Antarctica is the only continent without reptiles or snakes.

172. February 1865 is the only month in recorded history to not have a full moon.

173. Lightning strikes the earth 100 times every second.

174. It is physically impossible to lick your own elbow.

175. The average person's heart beats over 100,000 times per day!

176. Women blink nearly twice as often as men.

177. Horses can't vomit.

178. Penguins can jump up to 6-feet in the air.

179. All polar bears are left-handed.

180. Slugs have 4 noses.

181. It's possible to lead a cow upstairs, but not downstairs!

182. Rats multiply so quickly that after 18-months, 2 rats could have 1-million descendants!

183. The official name for a pregnant goldfish is a "twit."

184. Emus and Kangaroos can't walk backwards and were chosen to be on the Australian Coat of Arms specifically for that reason!

185. Only female mosquitos bite.

186. The microwave was invented after a researcher walked past a radar tube and the chocolate bar in his pocket melted.

187. A Boeing 767 is made up of over 3-million different parts.

188. In 1980, the only country in the world without telephones was Bhutan.

189. The official name for the dot above an 'i' is known as a "tittle".

190. Honey is the only food that does not spoil.

191. Coca cola was originally green.

192. The average American consumes 600 cans of soda each year.

193. In the United States, a pound of potato chips costs two-hundred times more than a pound of potatoes!

194. More than 2-billion pencils are made in the U.S. each year. If they were laid end to end, they would circle the world 9 times over!

195. Over 1-billion people live on less than $1 a day.

196. The Vatican City drinks more wine per capita than any other country at 74 liters per citizen, per year.

197. Roughly 40,000 Americans are injured by toilets every year.

198. No square piece of paper can be folded in half more than 7 times.

199. The official name for the hashtag on your keyboard (#) is called an octotroph.

200. The Declaration of Independence was written on hemp paper.

201. There are more plastic flamingos in the U.S. than real ones.

202. M&Ms stand for "Mars and Murries", the surnames of the founders.

203. Both Albert Einstein and Charles Darwin married their cousins.

204. More Monopoly money is printed each year than actual U.S. currency.

205. The scientific term for brain freeze is "sphenopalatine ganglioneuralgia."

206. Canadians say "sorry" so much that in 2009 they passed a law declaring that an apology couldn't be used in court as an admission of guilt.

207. A single strand of spaghetti is known as a "spaghetto".

208. At birth, a baby panda is smaller than a mouse!

209. The spiked dog collar was invented by the Ancient Greeks to protect their dogs from wolf attacks!

210. 75% of the world's diet consists of 12 plant species, and 5 animal species!

211. IKEA is an acronym that stands for Ingvar Kamprad Elmtaryd Agunnaryd, which is the founders name, farm where he grew up, and his hometown!

212. The youngest Pope in history was Pope Benedict IX who was only 11 years old when first elected.

213. In World War II Germany tried to destroy the British economy by dropping millions of counterfeit bills over London.

214. The color red doesn't actually make bulls angry. Bulls are colorblind.

215. Herring fish communicate by farting.

216. Prior to 2016, the song "Happy Birthday" was copyrighted and you had to pay a license to use it.

217. In the wild, mice live an average of 6 months. However, when kept as a pet they can live for up to 2 years!

218. The smell of rain comes from a unique mix of plant oils, bacteria, and ozone.

219. If you heat up a magnet, it loses its magnetism.

220. An average of 200 people die on board cruise ships each year.

221. The world's oldest unopened bottle of wine was found in a Roman tomb and is over 1,650 years old!

222. Tic Tacs got their name as a result of the sound they make when you shake the container.

223. A bolt of lightning can reach a temperature of 53,540 degrees Fahrenheit. That's 5 times hotter than the surface of the sun!

224. 4 Nile crocodiles have been found in Florida. They are the world's second largest species of crocodile and are far more dangerous than alligators.

225. There are over 820 different native languages spoken in Papua New Guinea! That represents 12% of the world's total number of languages.

226. Between North and South Korea there is a 155-mile space of land that is unoccupied by humans, and is home to some rare animal species!

227. Adult cats only meow at humans, not other cats. Kittens will meow to their mothers, but once they reach adulthood they stop!

228. Volvo invented the 3-point seatbelt. They then gave away the design for free, deeming it to be too important to keep to themselves.

229. If you add all of the numbers on a roulette wheel together, you end up with 666.

230. The thumbs-up symbol is thought to have been created by Chinese pilots who used it to communicate with ground staff at airports.

231. There is a volcano on Mars named Olympic Mons that stands at 2.5 times the height of Mount Everest!

232. When Dinosaurs roamed the earth, they lived on every continent except for Antarctica!

233. A blue whale's heart can weigh up to 1000lbs!

234. Before being accepted, J.K. Rowling's Harry Potter series was rejected by 12 different publishers!

235. There are over 6,000 different species of grass.

236. Ant queens can live for up to 30 years.

237. A group of lemurs is known as a conspiracy of lemurs.

238. Roughly 1/3 of cats have no reaction to catnip.

239. Elephants appear to consider humans "cute", in the same way humans think that puppies are cute.

240. A tall chef's hat is called a "toque".

241. In the U.S. each person owns an average of 7 pairs of blue jeans.

242. The Bible has been translated to over 3,000 languages, including fictional languages such as Elvish and Klingon.

243. Canada eats more macaroni and cheese than any other country in the world.

244. Alaska used to be the property of Russia, until it was purchased by the United States in 1866 for $7.2 million!

245. Sudan has 255 pyramids which is more than any other country!

246. Snakes can sense an upcoming earthquake from up to 75 miles away, and 5 days before they actually happen!

247. Animals yawn differently depending on their brain size. The bigger their brain, the longer they yawn!

248. Approximately 1 in every 2000 babies is born with teeth.

249. December 3rd is known as "Roof over your head day" and is a day to be grateful of everything you have in life!

250. There are more Lego mini-figures than actual people on earth.

251. The only difference between kosher salt and table salt is the size of salt grains. They both come from underground deposits.

252. Q-Tips were created in 1923 and were originally called Baby Gays.

253. When water freezes as an ice cube, it increases in volume by 9%.

254. Consuming grapefruit can restrict the effects of 43 different kinds of medication. It can even make caffeine stay in your bloodstream for longer.

255. Only 2% of the world's population has green eyes.

256. The odds of being born on the 29th of February are 1 in 1461.

257. At any given time, roughly 75% of houses in the United States contain at least 1 jar of peanut butter.

258. Cranes are built using cranes.

259. In every scene of the movie "Fight Club", there is a Starbucks coffee cup.

260. A cluster of bananas is called "a hand" and a single banana is called "a finger".

261. Saturn is so big that Earth could fit in it a total of 755 times!

262. A snail can sleep for up to 3 years.

Conclusion

Thanks again for choosing this book!

I hope you've enjoyed learning about all of these fun and random facts! Be sure to share them with your friends and family, and impressive them with your new knowledge.

www.ingramcontent.com/pod-product-compliance
Lightning Source LLC
LaVergne TN
LVHW021739060526
838200LV00052B/3371